T0197381

Kids can entrepreneur too!

...learning life + business skills

Yejide Akiode

AuthorHouse™ UK
1663 Liberty Drive
Bloomington, IN 47403 USA
www.authorhouse.co.uk
UK TFN: 0800 0148641 (Toll Free inside the UK)
UK Local: 02036 956322 (+44 20 3695 6322 from outside the UK)

Because of the dynamic nature of the Internet, any web addresses or links contained in this book may have changed
since publication and may no longer be valid. The views expressed in this work are solely those of the author and do
not necessarily reflect the views of the publisher, and the publisher hereby disclaims any responsibility for them.

Any people depicted in stock imagery provided by Getty Images are models,
and such images are being used for illustrative purposes only.
Certain stock imagery © Getty Images.

This book is printed on acid–free paper.

ISBN: 978–1–7283–5301–2 (sc)
ISBN: 978–1–7283–5300–5 (e)

Print information available on the last page.

Published by AuthorHouse 10/16/2020

authorHOUSE®

Contents

My Motivation

As a child, I never knew I had the qualities of an entrepreneur. The only quality I knew I had was that I was self-driven, but I didn't think much of it. Nor was I encouraged to hone or appreciate it. In hindsight, I realise that being self-driven and highly decisive have been major reasons for my success in business and in life. My skills have also been fattened by a healthy diet of books and taking part in various training programmes.

I started this campaign of letting kids discover and appreciate their latent talents and innate abilities that are often not acknowledged or celebrated. We have focused on goals 8 and 12 of the sustainable development goals and strongly believe that entrepreneurship should be taught in schools because of the skills that can be discovered and mindsets that can developed along the way.

Rt Hon. Anne Milton, former MP for Guildford, House of Commons, London, lends her voice by saying,

"Entrepreneurial education offers so many benefits for children from all backgrounds. It is a chance to develop and exercise skills that can't be learnt easily in the classroom. We all want to see young people developing the skills to make them the entrepreneurs of the future"

I implore every parent to give their kids opportunities to shine and put them on the path of success. Join us as we raise a new community of self-confident kidpreneurs!

Introduction

Did you know that the word 'entrepreneur' is said to have been coined by an economist called Jean-Baptiste Say? It was derived from an old French word, *entreprendre* which means an undertaker or adventurer.

Another definition of an entrepreneur is simply someone who owns a business and grows it. I believe an entrepreneur is someone who spots an opportunity and takes the necessary actions to make it work. Though these definitions are accurate, there is a whole lot to this big word called 'entrepreneur'.

It is said that entrepreneurs are born with 5 per cent innate talents (nature) and 95 per cent made through trainings and life experiences (nurture).

Do you think you have some innate talents to be an entrepreneur? I believe everyone does.

Do you think you can learn the skills that make one an entrepreneur? I believe everyone can.

We will explore the skills and tricks that make one a successful entrepreneur using a simple and easy to remember acronym—E.N.T.R.E.P.R.E.N.E.U.R. We included stories of various entrepreneurs and 'kidpreneurs', - the name we have given kid entrepreneurs. For us, the word 'entrepreneur' is more than a noun; we have regarded it as a verb.

Look out for the Kidpreneur quotes at the end of every chapter. Have fun with the word search challenges, scrambled words, quick quizzes, and assessments.

Let's dive in.

What's Inside?

E   — *Enjoy what you do.* What am I passionate about?

N   — *Never stop trying.* Can I believe in myself even when others do not believe in me?

T   — *Time management leads to progress and success.* How do I get all I need to do done?

R   — *Resilience lets you bounce back.* Do I have the spring to bounce back and keep trying?

E   — *Ethical business practices can make you stand apart.* Can business be done right?

P   — *Problem-solving skills are vital.* How do I solve big problems?

R   — *Relational skills help you deal with people.* How do I make a first good impression?

E   — *Enterprising opportunities are out there.* How can I spot business opportunities?

N   — *Never stop learning.* How do I open myself to continuous learning?

E   — *Earn some money.* Can I make, spend, and save money all at the same time?

U   — *Unique creativity is in everyone.* How can I identify my unique skills and talents?

R   — *Refusal skills are a 'must'.* How can I say no when pressured to engage in unhealthy and risky behavior?

Quick Facts

Tech Entrepreneur—Steven Paul Jobs
Co-founder—Apple Incorporated

Born 24 February 1955. He was adopted by Paul and Clara Jobs, whom he always considered to be his real parents.

Do you know that his love for electronics and technology started when he was age ten? This led to a lifelong interest in electronics and design.

At age thirteen, he was offered a summer job at Hewlett Packard after he called Bill Packard to ask for parts for an electronics project.

He and a partner, Steve Wozniak, founded Apple Inc., makers of the iPhone, iPad, iPod, and other products.

Skill 1

E, the first letter in the word
E.N.T.R.E.P.R.E.N.E.U.R., stands for ...

Enjoy what you do.

An entrepreneur must enjoy what he or she does. An entrepreneur must be passionate about it.

Being passionate means to have an intense desire and a strong and almost uncontrollable emotion about something—in this case, an idea or a cause. Have you ever had such a feeling?

Steve Jobs said,

> You've got to find what you love, do what you believe is great work. Keep looking; don't settle. Sometimes life's going to hit you in the head with a brick. Don't lose faith. I'm convinced that the only thing that kept me going was that I loved what I did.

Little wonder he was listed as an inventor of more than 340 technology and design patents.

Kidpreneur Quote

You must be passionate and love what you do
because PASSION precedes any form of PROFIT!

ACTIVITY

HOW CAN YOU IDENTIFY YOUR PASSION? THESE FEW QUESTIONS COULD HELP...

- What do you love to do and hate to stop doing?

  _____
  _____
  _____

- When you are in a bookstore, what section of the store are you naturally drawn to?

  _____
  _____
  _____

- What website(s) do you often visit?

  _____
  _____
  _____

- What is your favourite TV programme?

  _____
  _____
  _____

Quick Facts

Author/Entrepreneur—J. K. Rowling
Author—*Harry Potter* Series

J. K. Rowling was born 31 July 1965 in England. J. K. Rowling is a pen name. Her real name is Joanne Rowling.

She started writing stories at the age of six. Her first book was titled *Rabbits*.

She got the idea of Harry Potter while on a crowded train travelling from Manchester. Though she was broke, she enrolled in writing classes. Her writing was rejected countless times by publishers until Bloomsbury decided to publish her work.

Over 500 million copies of her books have been sold, making *Harry Potter* the best-selling book series in history, and she is said to be the first author billionaire.

Harry Potter and the Philosopher's Stone, published in 1995, was her first book.

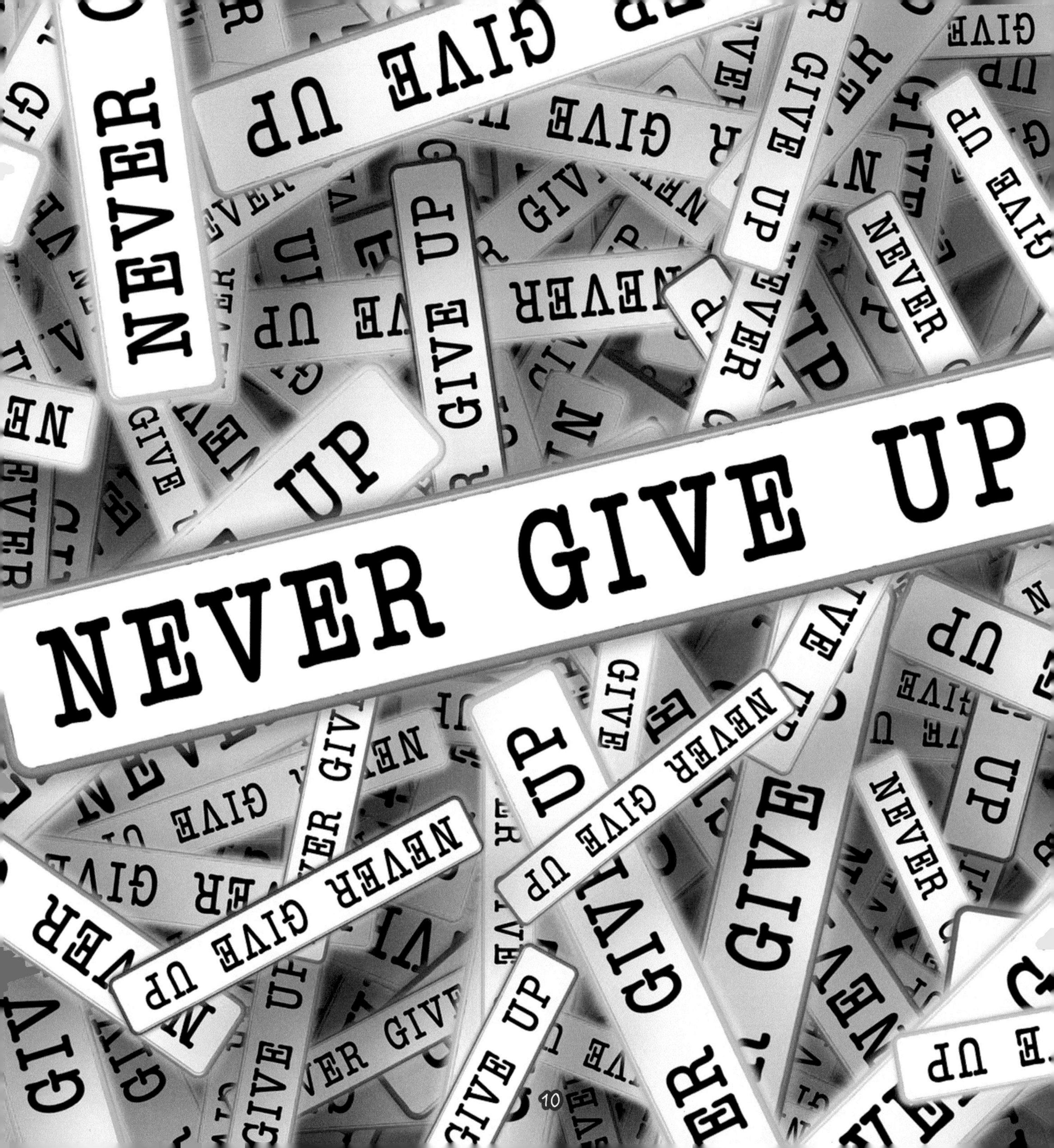
NEVER GIVE UP

Skill 2

N, the second letter in the word
E.N.T.R.E.P.R.E.N.E.U.R., stands for ...

Never stop trying.

Have there been times when you tried some sums in maths and gave up because they seemed too hard? Or do you keep trying until you're good at it?

Has someone—a friend, parent, sibling, or teacher—told you that you cannot do this or that? You've probably heard that many times. Is what *they* say more important than what *you* say or believe?

Most ideas started as a big dream that people thought could not be possible. They include the invention of the light bulb, the airplane, and even Uber—the taxi company.

Believe in yourself and in your dreams!

Kidpreneur Quote

Even when it's rough and tough, true
entrepreneurs never give up!

ACTIVITY 1
WORD SEARCH CHALLENGE

D	Q	W	E	R	T	Y	T	I	O	P	P	N
P	S	D	F	Y	R	R	A	H	F	V	O	L
H	D	F	B	O	N	V	C	X	S	I	B	N
I	D	F	O	C	U	S	X	Z	T	B	C	F
L	E	B	F	B	H	Y	I	A	J	N	S	R
O	F	V	B	Q	W	E	N	Y	I	O	K	E
S	F	A	B	G	N	I	F	S	V	Q	D	H
O	V	G	S	N	M	B	C	S	V	Q	G	S
P	B	P	A	R	G	H	K	N	S	C	V	I
H	M	O	E	N	O	T	S	C	B	N	M	L
E	J	T	V	G	F	V	R	W	F	B	S	B
R	E	T	F	F	E	W	T	G	D	G	N	U
D	Q	E	B	D	S	D	V	B	N	Q	S	P
H	Y	R	O	W	L	I	N	G	D	S	F	X

Book	Focus	Joanne	Harry	Publisher
Stone	Determination	Rowling	Potter	Philosopher

ACTIVITY 2
THINK UP A SKILL THAT STARTS WITH THE LETTER N

N_____

Quick Facts

Confectionery Entrepreneur—Alina Morse
Founder —Zollipops

She came up with the idea for a lollipop created from healthy ingredients. It was not just good for you but good to eat.

Born in 2005, Alina started the business at age nine, after getting the idea at the bank.

Alina wanted to make a difference and help people stay away from sugar, which is bad for the teeth. She and her dad made the first batch of healthy suckers after doing much research from dentists and hygienists.

Now fourteen years old, Alina effectively manages her time between her schoolwork, dance classes, and her business.

Skill 3

T, the third letter in the word
E.N.T.R.E.P.R.E.N.E.U.R., stands for ...

Time management leads to progress and success.

Being an entrepreneur comes with some rewards. One of which is time to spend with family, friends, and some fun activities too. However, a basic quality an entrepreneur must have is the ability to manage or make good use of his or her time.

Learn from Alina Morse, the CEO of Zollipops. She effectively manages her time as a student, a dancer, and a business owner. You, too, can learn to manage your time well.

How to Manage Your Time

Use a *To*-do list or daily planner; make this a habit.
*I*nsist on following through on every task, and give yourself a deadline for each task.
Work on the *M*ost important to least important tasks.
*E*liminate (get rid of) every form of procrastination.

Benefits of Time Management

*T*remendous progress is made.
*I*mproved organisation and planning achieved.
*M*ore time for other fun activities.
*E*liminate (get rid of) or lessen stress.

Kidpreneur Quote

Down on Paper is half-way done.
Write your daily activities down!

ACTIVITY 1

DESIGN YOUR PLANNER & PLAN YOUR WEEKEND
SAMPLE PLANNER

DAYS	7-9AM	9-11AM	11-1PM	1-3PM	3-5PM	5-7PM
FRIDAY						
SATURDAY						
SUNDAY						

ACTIVITY 2

WORD SEARCH CHALLENGE

Q	W	E	R	T	U	I	O	P	J	N	P	L
W	R	Q	T	E	T	R	Y	U	I	O	O	T
F	H	A	S	D	O	F	H	J	L	I	T	M
V	D	Q	Z	B	D	C	D	F	G	T	N	B
Q	Z	M	A	N	O	V	X	H	J	A	E	A
A	S	Z	O	L	L	I	P	O	P	S	M	D
S	D	F	E	M	I	T	G	P	L	I	E	E
F	D	S	F	S	S	N	R	Q	A	N	G	F
G	P	D	G	D	T	O	A	W	N	A	A	N
H	P	F	E	F	G	G	N	E	N	G	N	M
J	F	G	R	R	G	D	F	R	E	R	A	J
K	G	B	E	H	H	F	E	S	R	O	M	K
L	B	S	G	U	N	V	F	T	D	F	N	O
M	S	R	U	O	V	A	L	F	C	D	G	R
N	N	M	H	O	M	B	G	Y	O	W	F	P
B	T	J	J	J	Y	N	R	U	P	A	D	C
C	Y	K	U	T	U	Y	Y	I	H	N	V	A

Alina	Zollipops	Morse	Flavours	Planner
Organisation	Todolist	Management	Progress	Time

ACTIVITY 3

QUICK QUIZ

Where did she get the idea?

_____

Quick Facts

Inventor and Designer—James Dyson
Founder—Dyson LTD.

When he got frustrated with his family's vacuum, he set out to invent a better version in 1978. It took him fifteen years and 5,126 failed samples to create the world's first bagless vacuum.

Born in May 1947, James attended art school in London and later earned an engineering degree.

James said, "I made 5,127 prototypes [samples] of my vacuum before I got it right. There were 5,126 failures but I learned from each one. That's how I came up with a solution, I don't mind failures."

Now, Dyson units are used in many homes and public restrooms. He has created many things, from vacuums to hand dryers, and he is now working on electric cars!

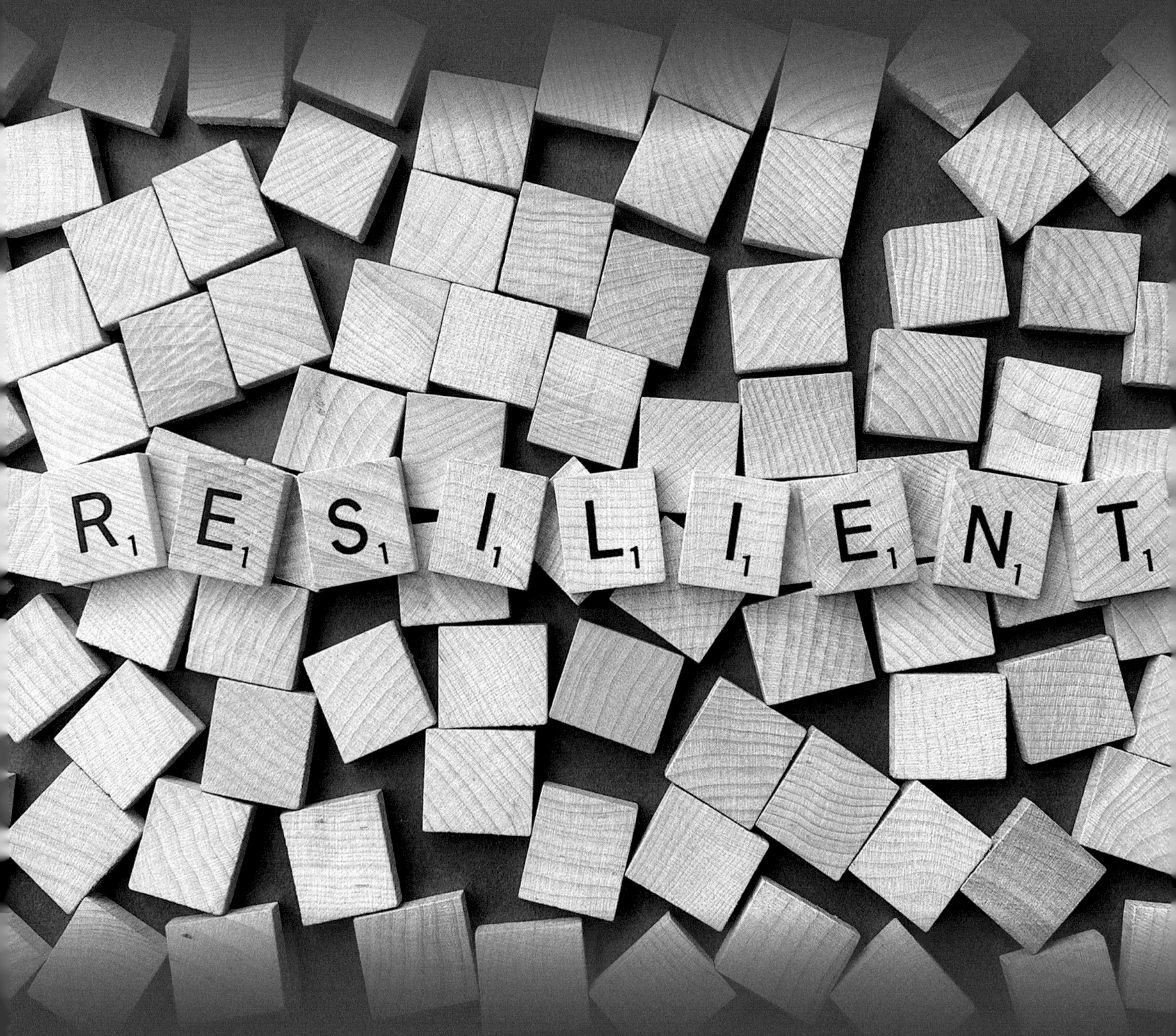
R1 E1 S1 I1 L1 I1 E1 N1 T1

Skill 4

R, the fourth letter in the word
E.N.T.R.E.P.R.E.N.E.U.R., stands for ...

Resilience lets you bounce back.

This is a major quality or attribute of entrepreneurs. Resilience is the ability to make mistakes, learn from them, and move on. It's called bouncebackability.

Hence, even when you feel deflated—perhaps after failing at a task, you need to retain some air (self-belief) within to be able to bounce back. Have you ever seen a deflated ball bounce?

Also, have you ever wondered why cobwebs can be found at the highest points of a palace, a prison, or a pantry? It is because spiders are resilient and do not give up. Take down their webs—which are their homes—and they will build new, stronger ones within hours. They will succeed or die trying!

How to Build Resilience
- *R*—Refuse to focus on failures and mistakes.
- *I*—Information must be sought to come up with possible solutions.
- *S*—Seek support and share with a trusted adult.
- *E*—Evaluate and make a final decision.

Kidpreneur Quote

We believe in failing, getting up
and moving forward.

ACTIVITY 1
HOW CAN YOU BUILD RESILIENCE? MENTION 2 POINTS...

1. _____
   _____

2. _____
   _____

ACTIVITY 2
UNSCRAMBLE THESE WORDS

- Ottotype: _____
- Aumvcu: _____
- Ceisrinlee: _____
- Rieflau: _____
- Radsiitnlu: _____
- Ergsdnie: _____
- Rnitnvoe: _____
- Easjm: _____
- Osdny: _____
- Episrd: _____

Inventor	James	Vacuum	Prototype	Designer
Industrial	Spider	Dyson	Failure	Resilience

ACTIVITY 3
THINK UP A SKILL THAT STARTS WITH THE LETTER R

R_____

Quick Facts

Budding Kidpreneur—Mikaila Ulmer
Founder—Me and the Bees Lemonade

Mikaila was born in 2005 in Austin, Texas, to D'Andran and Theo Ulmer, who both have business degrees.

Stung twice by a bee at the age of four, Mikaila became fascinated with honeybees. Her parents encouraged her to make a product for a children's business fair, and she made lemonade.

Mikaila took her great-grandmother's flaxseed lemonade recipe and added local honey to it. She donates the profits to help efforts to save the dying bee population.

Mikaila received $60,000 (£45,000) on *Shark Tank* to grow Me & the Bees Lemonade.

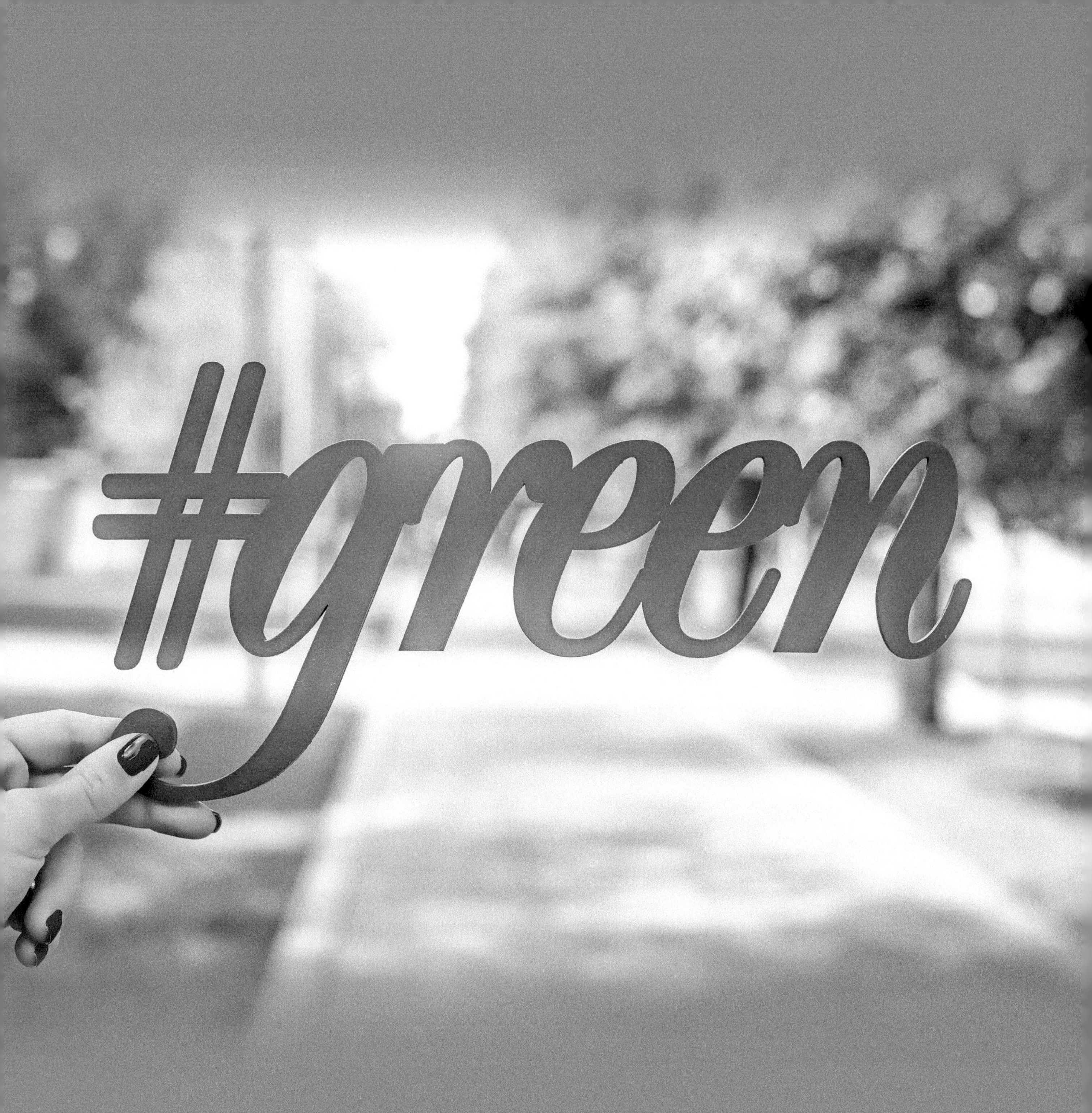
#green

Skill 5

E, the fifth letter in the word
E.N.T.R.E.P.R.E.N.E.U.R., stands for ...

Ethical business practices can make you stand apart.

Running a business is more than making profit. It is about doing things right. It is also important to know that it reflects who you are and what you think is important.

Have you heard of the sustainable development goals (SDGs)?

Well they are a collection of seventeen global goals designed to achieve a better and happy environment in the future for everyone.

Goal 12 of the sustainable development goals is, 'Responsible consumption and production', which can be achieved by using eco-friendly methods and reducing the amount of waste.

As Kidpreneurs, using recyclable products such as aluminium, glass, or paper to sell your lemonade, ice cream, or popcorn would be doing a lot of good to the environment. Recycling your wastes can help conserve the earth and make it a better place to live in.

Giving back to the environment or community is also important.

Mikaila Ulmer found out through a research assignment that the honeybee population was dying and set out to create a business to save the honeybee population. A portion of her profits still goes to this.

Kidpreneur Quote

Our 'Profits' must profit the Planet.

ACTIVITY 1
QUICK QUIZ

1. What is the 12th goal of the SDGs'

   _____

2. What does SDG mean?

   _____

3. How can you help the environment? Name 2 ways...
   a. _____
   b. _____

4. Mention 3 recyclable products
   a. _____
   b. _____
   c. _____

5. What is Mikaila Ulmer's mission?

   _____

ACTIVITY 2
DO YOU HAVE COMMUNITY PROJECT IDEAS? A FEW EXAMPLES ARE:
- Collect old stuffed animals and dolls, clean up or repair them, then donate them.
- Collect old clothes and shoes and donate them
- Pick up litter around the park

Write about your community project idea and how you intend to carry it out.

Quick Facts

Inventor/Designer—Mark Publicover
Founder—Jumpsport Inc.

Born in 1958, Mark Publicover earned a degree in economics.

Entrepreneurs George Nissen, a gymnastics and diving competitor, and his gymnastics coach, Larry Griswold, invented the trampoline in 1936. However, as the popularity of the trampoline grew, so did the number of accidents.

When Mark Publicover's young neighbour hurt herself when she fell off the trampoline while jumping with his children, he began building samples of his safety net enclosure designs.

The first safety net enclosure was sold in 1997, almost sixty years after the invention of the trampoline. Since then, trampoline accidents have been reduced approximately 50 per cent. Almost all new trampolines are sold with safety net enclosures.

Skill 6

P, the sixth letter in the word
E.N.T.R.E.P.R.E.N.E.U.R., stands for ...

Problem—solving skills are vital.

We all face several problems every day, ranging from falling out with friends, problems on the sports field, or academic challenges. Yet many young people do not know how to solve these problems. Problem-solving is a skill that improves our thinking, creativity, independence, and self-confidence. It might also interest you to know that entrepreneurs are problem-solvers. They see a problem as an opportunity and proffer a solution to it, just like Mark Publicover did.

"How can I solve a problem?" you might ask.

The following 4-step problem-solving technique is effective.

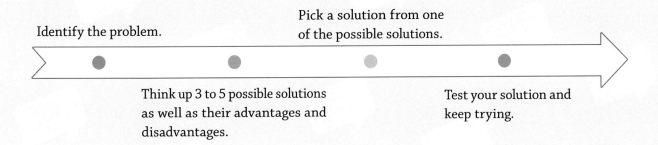

Identify the problem.

Pick a solution from one of the possible solutions.

Think up 3 to 5 possible solutions as well as their advantages and disadvantages.

Test your solution and keep trying.

Kidpreneur Quote

KEEP CALM! With every problem
comes a solution

BELOW IS A LIST OF PROBLEMS THAT NEED SOLUTIONS. GIVE THREE TO FIVE SOLUTIONS FOR EACH PROBLEM USING THE TECHNIQUE ABOVE

Problem 1: Forgetting to bring my Kidpreneur Klub folder on Thursdays
Possible solutions:

1. _____
2. _____
3. _____
4. _____
5. _____

Best solution to try and why.

_____
_____

Problem 2: Bullying and falling out with friends.
Possible solutions:

1. _____
2. _____
3. _____
4. _____
5. _____

Best solution to try and why.

_____
_____

Problem 3: Not doing my homework before due date.
Possible solutions:

1. _____
2. _____
3. _____
4. _____
5. _____

Best solution to try and why.

_____

_____

Quick Facts

**The Socks Kids—Sebastian and Brandon Martinez
Founders—Are You Kidding?**

In June 2013, his mum randomly asked him if he would like to design his own socks, and in May 2014, Sebastian became the CEO of Are You Kidding? He was just six years old.

Young Sebastian was always happy to receive a pair of socks as a gift. He had more than one hundred pairs of colourful and wacky designed socks by age five.

Brandon quickly earned the title 'director of sales', and the company recorded its first sales that day with tens of thousands of socks sold to date.

However, Sebastian was a bit shy and couldn't speak with strangers. So his brother, Brandon, was called to help. Brandon immediately dazzled the customers and had them buying lots of socks!

Skill 7

R, the seventh letter in the word
E.N.T.R.E.P.R.E.N.E.U.R., stands for ...

Relational skills help you deal with people.

Your ability to relate with people and treat them right is an extremely positive attribute to have or develop. In business, this is called 'customer service'. As a kidpreneur, if you have an amazing business idea and made a nice, fancy product, are you guaranteed to have a successful business? Definitely not. You cannot be in business without customers.

How can you present yourself in a confident manner and make a good impression?

According to June Hines Moore, a simple way to present yourself to others and make a good impression goes by these 'Six Ss', and they stand for the following:

Stand: Always stand to meet or greet someone who is standing.
Smile: A smile goes a mile.
See their eyes: Politely look a person in their eyes.
Shake hands: A firm handshake is generally accepted as a polite form of greeting.
Say your name "Hello, my name is [insert your name]. It's nice to meet you."
Say the other person's name: For instance, you can simply say, "Hello [insert the person's name]. I'm [your name]. It's nice to meet you too."

Kidpreneur Quote

Treat everyone equally regardless of
age, appearance and attitude

ACTIVITY 1
PRACTICE THE 6-STEP INTRODUCTION

Stand

Smile

See their eyes

Shake hands

Say your name

Say the other person's name

ACTIVITY 2
WORD SEARCH CHALLENGE

T	A	Q	R	T	H	S	K	C	E	S
S	O	C	K	S	E	B	F	G	L	E
D	S	X	A	C	L	F	D	A	I	B
F	F	F	S	Z	L	Q	Q	Z	M	A
S	V	E	L	P	O	E	P	X	S	S
E	K	A	H	S	D	N	A	H	H	T
R	B	H	B	B	B	F	F	D	F	I
V	H	H	N	N	S	H	F	D	R	A
I	R	E	M	O	T	S	U	C	G	N
C	N	N	M	M	A	B	V	G	B	J
E	R	M	R	H	N	N	G	H	E	K
L	W	F	N	O	D	N	A	R	B	B

Socks	Smile	Stand	Handshake	People
Customer	Sebastian	Brandon	Service	Hello

Quick Facts

Chinese Inspiration—Jack Ma
Founder—Alibaba, a China-Based
Business-to-Business Marketplace Site

Born 10 September 1964 in China as Ma Yun, he was nicknamed 'Jack' by a foreigner who couldn't pronounce his Chinese name.

He heard about the internet in 1994 and started his first company. He was further exposed to the internet by his friends in the United States and realised that there was no information about China online.

He and a friend created a website related to China and received emails from Chinese investors roughly three hours after it was launched. Ma realised this was a great business opportunity, and with the help of his computer teacher, started his second company in 1995 and Alibaba in 1999.

42

Skill 8

E, the eighth letter in the word
E.N.T.R.E.P.R.E.N.E.U.R., stands for ...

Enterprising opportunities are out there.

An 'enterprise' is simply another name for a business, but the word 'enterprising' is used to describe someone who sees an opportunity and takes the necessary actions or initiatives to make it work even if it seems difficult.

It is about being proactive and having a positive attitude in any given situation. This is also an important quality to have as a student.

How to spot opportunities?

- Keep your eyes open.
- Have an active mind.
- Think through problems.
- Embrace and learn from mistakes.
- Stay positive.

Kidpreneur Quote

We believe like Richard Branson that
Business opportunities are like buses,
there's always another one coming.

WORD SEARCH CHALLENGE

F	Q	C	W	E	T	Y	U	I	O	K	P	L	K	J
G	R	H	M	Q	X	C	V	B	G	C	H	J	K	M
V	E	I	B	A	L	I	B	A	B	A	X	Q	F	B
N	T	N	C	V	B	N	N	B	M	J	G	S	C	V
M	U	A	X	V	N	T	U	V	M	G	E	S	C	Q
I	P	P	A	G	B	E	V	M	E	N	K	O	L	P
K	M	E	N	T	E	R	P	R	I	S	E	B	M	Z
S	O	V	S	S	E	N	I	S	U	B	T	R	Q	V
D	C	V	B	N	Z	E	C	F	R	Y	J	O	D	S
S	Y	J	I	V	F	T	B	I	A	B	D	C	R	G
S	E	I	T	I	N	U	T	R	O	P	P	O	H	S

China	Jack	Ma	Enterprise	Internet
Alibaba	Opportunities	Computer	Investors	Business

ACTIVITY 2
WHAT 3 WAYS CAN I SPOT OPPORTUNITIES?

1. _____
2. _____
3. _____

ACTIVITY 3
QUICK QUIZ

- What was Jack Ma's real name?

  _____

- Where was he exposed to the internet?

  _____

- What year did he start his first business?

  _____

Quick Facts

Tech Enterpreneur—Mark Zuckerberg
Founder—Facebook

Born 14 May 1984, Mark, developed an interest in computers at an early age. To keep up with his increasing interest in computers, a private computer tutor was hired by his parents. He also began to take graduate courses at a college near his home.

Although he enrolled and dropped out of Harvard University, his fascination with and love for computers was amazing, and he has continued learning and working on developing new programmes.

Although he had other business ideas while at university, Mark is now the CEO of Facebook and one of the world's youngest billionaires.

Skill 9

N, the ninth letter in the word
E.N.T.R.E.P.R.E.N.E.U.R., stands for ...

Never stop learning.

The solution to a bold, bright, and brilliant future is continuous learning. As a student and kidpreneur, it is important to stay informed about constant changes in the world. Personal development and self-learning are vital. Learning could be *formal* through attending college, university, or taking online courses. It could also be *informal*, acquired through reading books and newspapers, watching documentaries and biographies, or learning from an adult. Reading this book proves that you're a learner. Well done!

Mark Zuckerberg, along with many other successful entrepreneurs, figured this out.

Businesspeople have business mentors, and top kidpreneurs in the United States—including Moziah Bridges (CEO of Mo's Bows) and Ryan Kelly (CEO of Ry's Ruffery)—have their mothers as their 'momagers'. Mum, manager, and probably mentor all in one.

Benefits of continuous learning

1. When you grow, your business grows.
2. It makes you valuable and relevant.
3. It makes you more skilful and a better person.
4. It keeps you updated on current happenings around you and in the bigger world.

Kidpreneur Quote

From Business books to Business Mentors –
You need to keep learning and keep growing!

ACTIVITY 1
QUICK QUIZ

- What is the name of Mark Zuckerberg's company?
  - a. Facemash
  - b. Facebook
  - c. Facenote

- When did he get interested in computers?
  - a. At an early age
  - b. When he was born
  - c. When he graduated from Harvard

- Mention 2 types of learning
  1. _____
  2. _____

- Mention 2 benefits of continuous learning
  1. _____
  2. _____

ACTIVITY 2
UNSCRAMBLE THESE WORDS

- OKOFCBEA   _____
- UEBKERRZG   _____
- LNGEARNI   _____
- MKAR   _____
- OUTPERCMS   _____
- ARRVDHA   _____
- NLIOAIBILRE   _____

Quick Facts

The Bow Tie Guy—Moziah Bridges
Founder—Mo's Bows

Moziah was born in 2001. When he was four years old, he loved to wear a suit and tie and he insisted on dressing himself when possible.

Moziah started his business when he was nine years old. It was born from his love for fashion and bow ties. He was unhappy with the bow tie selection available for kids his age. He said, "I like to wear bow ties because they make me look good and feel good."

Moziah Bridges has built himself an extremely successful business and continues to earn good money.

Skill 10

E, the tenth letter in the word
E.N.T.R.E.P.R.E.N.E.U.R., stands for ...

Earn some money.

Wouldn't it be nice to have some pocket money, so you could buy some fancy things you like?

How do you think you can do that? Well you can earn money by doing more work at home or harder house chores. You can also earn some money by starting a business, like Moziah Bridges.

You can do this by using your skills or strengths (baking, caring for animals, organising), things you own (your bicycle for quick deliveries, your computer for building websites or coding), or school subjects you love (arts—drawing wall art or handcrafted cards; English language—blogging or writing books).

You also need to know ...

- What it means to plan your money. Record all the money you make and make a list of important things you need to buy or do. This is a form of bookkeeping and budgeting.

- What it means to keep some money, too, in a piggy bank or an actual bank. This is called savings.

Kidpreneur Quote

Everyone can make money; Little
kids can have big ideas too

ACTIVITY 1

WRITE YOUR 3 TOP REASONS FOR WANTING TO MAKE MORE MONEY OR STARTING A BUSINESS?

1. _____
2. _____
3. _____

ACTIVITY 2

LET'S SOLVE THIS BUDGETING PROBLEM

Harry is going to 7th grade and desires to get himself a bike. He gets £20 a week and uses £2 everyday (Monday to Friday) for his school lunches. The bike he really loves would cost him £100.

- How much would Harry spend per week?

_____

- How much would Harry save per week?

_____

- How many weeks would Harry need to save to buy the bike?

_____

ACTIVITY 3

DRAW UP IN THE LIST BELOW ALL THE MONEY YOU HAVE AND WHAT YOU WANT TO BUY OR SAVE

Money I have (income)	Things to buy (expenses)	Amount to save

Quick Facts

YouTube Sensation—Amber Kelley
Founder—*Cook with Amber*

Born in 2003, Amber was teased in school about her healthy snacks. Instead of letting it get her down, it sparked her creative side with the phrase, 'Being healthy is cool.' She was also partly inspired by her parents, who are wellness coaches.

Amber became famous with her cooking for kids show. She was featured on Jamie Oliver's Food Channel programme and won the first season of the Food Network's *Star Kids*.

Amber is a cookbook author, speaker, has her own web series on Food Network, and has over 45,000 YouTube subscribers.

Skill 11

U, the eleventh letter in the word
E.N.T.R.E.P.R.E.N.E.U.R., stands for ...

Unique creativity is in everyone.

It is worth stating that you are not a mass-produced copy but a God-created original. Just like your fingerprints are unique to you, so are your talents. But how can you identify your uniqueness you may ask.

You can understand your uniqueness—or hint of a business idea—through the following:

- *Skills and Strengths:* These are your abilities to do something well, such as baking, organising, or calligraphy. Amber liked to cook. It could also be a good quality or feature you have, such as your voice, face, or style.
- *Something You Own:* Your belongings—such as your bicycle, computer, smoothie maker, sewing machine, piano—can help you realise your creative side.
- *School Subjects You Love:* Which subjects are you good at? There are creative ways to use writing, maths, coding, art, and many other subjects.

You also need to be creative in promoting your business. As a kidpreneur, you must:

- Find the right customers (people). Who are you targeting? For example, storybooks for children or bracelets for girls.
- Reach them the right way (place). Where would you sell your product or service. For example, having an ice cream stall at the park or simply going door to door.
- Choose the right method (promotion). How would you promote your business? Some examples are colourful flyers and posters, and websites.
- Choose the right words (product). What value are you giving your product or service? The words you use should express that value: for example, 'fresh', 'simple', 'yummy', 'handmade', 'shiny', 'pure', 'quality', and so on.
- Decide on the right cost (price). How much are you charging for it. For example, $5 per bracelet, £1.50 per book marker. Consider your one-time expenses and ongoing expenses. And don't forget the cost of your time.

Kidpreneur Quote

Everyone is unique and gifted!

ACTIVITY
HOW CAN YOU IDENTIFY YOUR UNIQUE AND CREATIVE SELF?

Identifying a winning business idea could be as simple as starting with what you have. This way, you will save yourself a lot of time and start-up costs. Amber came up with a creative business idea after being teased about her healthy school snacks.

Let's dive into your **skills**, your **strengths**, **subjects** you love and **something** you own.

Skills...
What skills or talents have you been recognised for? (This includes compliments, awards, trophies, praise by your Parents, Teachers or Friends). _____

_____

Strengths...
What are your hobbies or things you do effortlessly without a lot of preparation?

_____

School Subjects loved...
What school subjects do you enjoy? Maths, English, Coding, Arts etc.

_____

_____

Something you own...
What do you or your parents own? – A piano, a bicycle, a computer, smoothie or sewing machine etc.

_____

_____

Quick Facts

**Double-Face and Snap Hair
Barrette Inventor—Gabby Goodwin
Founder—Gabby Bows**

Gabby started her business at age seven to solve the problem of her missing hair barrettes. Her mum decided it was time to solve that problem by inventing their own. Gabby and Mum invented the first patented double-face, double-snap barrettes.

Her barrettes have been sold in most states in the United States and in different countries too. She was also awarded the South Carolina Young Entrepreneur of the Year award in 2015.

She lives by the following quotes:

Believe in yourself so you can achieve whatever dreams you have!

A 'no' is just an abbreviation for 'Next Opportunity.'

Skill 12

R, the twelfth letter in the word
E.N.T.R.E.P.R.E.N.E.U.R., stands for …

Refusal skills are a 'must'.

This is the ability to say or show that you are unwilling to do what someone is requesting you to do, especially if it is something that could lead to bad results, by saying a firm but polite, "No", and standing by your decision.

It is also the ability to accept no—without feeling discouraged—when people refuse to budge to your sales tricks or gimmicks. Gabby's mum taught her to understand the word 'no' in business was simply an acronym for *Next Opportunity*.

Young people often find themselves in situations where others encourage them to do something that is clearly risky, illegal, or unhealthy. Unfortunately, too many end up giving in to this pressure, not because they really want to, but simply because they do not know how to respond in such situations. They are often also afraid of losing the other person's friendship or being left out. It takes a lot of confidence and courage to say no in the face of peer pressure. There are several ways in which you can say no.

- Firmly but politely make your standpoint clear by saying, "Thanks, but no thanks."
- Say something funny to lighten the mood and divert attention to something else.
- Use your body's non-verbal communication method—body language—to emphasise that you don't want to do something. This speaks louder than words. For example, walk away and refuse to discuss the matter any further to avoid continuous pressure.

Kidpreneur Quote

Learn to accept or say 'NO'. It does not
always mean never; it may simply mean
'Not now' or 'Next Opportunity'

ACTIVITY 1
MENTION 2 WAYS IN WHICH YOU CAN SAY 'NO' IN THE FACE OF PRESSURE

1. _____
2. _____

ACTIVITY 2
WORD SEARCH CHALLENGE

C	P	R	E	S	S	U	R	E	R	H	Y	U
S	O	D	W	Q	R	Y	U	I	O	T	H	P
D	L	M	A	N	A	G	E	M	E	N	T	G
F	I	G	M	G	H	D	F	H	H	F	L	U
B	T	F	H	U	M	E	E	B	N	L	A	T
G	E	V	J	N	C	H	N	J	A	E	R	
H	L	B	N	K	S	I	R	R	K	G	H	
M	Y	N	F	G	H	S	C	E	U	E	N	S
K	F	M	D	R	R	I	N	A	Y	L	U	
Y	S	J	R	W	L	O	J	Y	T	L	K	L
U	L	A	S	U	F	N	R	J	E	I	U	T
I	L	A	S	U	F	E	R	I	Q	J	O	L
O	G	G	E	B	P	D	W	F	V	G	N	N

Risk	Refusal	Illegal	Unhealthy	Pressure
Communication	Result	Management	Decision	Politely

ACTIVITY 3
ACCORDING TO GABBY'S MUM, THE WORD 'NO' COULD MEAN...

a. Nothing Yet

b. Next Opportunity

c. Never Stop

Conclusion

Helping kids to develop an entrepreneurial mindset means helping them to believe in themselves and to have big dreams for the future - a future with opportunities and possibilities. The earlier these skills are learned, the more they become second-nature.

I believe creativity is locked up in small packages waiting to be unwrapped. If these entrepreneurs and kidpreneurs can do it, so can you!

Success in business requires a couple of skills and tricks which can be learned and applied to make your business stand the test of time. As a kidpreneur, you will always need support from family and friends to help you juggle your schoolwork and have some fun too.

To start your business, we always advise the following:

- You must be excited about it.
- You must listen to your inner voice or feelings.
- You must be able to start it right away.
- You must have time for it, which means it can be done after school or on weekends.
- You can get help and support from your parents.
- It must not use more money than you already have—except if parents are willing to give you some more.

If you read through the book and completed all the exercises, great job!

Best wishes on your new adventure!

References For More Information

Steve Jobs	https://www.biography.com/business-figure/steve-jobs
J.K. Rowling	https://www.jkrowling.com/about/
Alina Morse	https://zollipops.com/our-story/
James Dyson	https://en.wikipedia.org/wiki/James_Dyson
Mikaila Ulmer	https://www.meandthebees.com/
Mark Publicover	https://www.jumpsport.com/about-us/
Sebastian and Brandon Martinez	https://areyoukiddingsocks.com/
Jack Ma	https://en.wikipedia.org/wiki/Jack_Ma
Mark Zuckerberg	https://www.biography.com/business-figure/mark-zuckerberg
Moziah Bridges	https://www.inc.com/larry-kim/this-12-year-old-ceo-runs-a-150k-business.html and https://mosbowsmemphis.com/
Amber Kelley	cookwithamber.com/
Gabby Goodwin	https://www.megbrunson.com/gabby-goodwin/ and https://gabbybows.com/

About the Author

Yejide Akiode is an author, educationist, a life coach, and a serial entrepreneur who holds a Master of Business Administration from Surrey Business School, University of Surrey. She also runs the Kidpreneur Klub®, where kids are taught life and business skills. This is her sixth book.

When she is not developing contents, you would likely find Yejide watching a movie, listening to an audio book, looking for a new recipe or checking out interior design videos.

Would you like to join the Kidpreneur Klub?
Sign up for our online course by visiting
www.myeduspace.co.uk.

Printed in the United States
By Bookmasters